The Fanatics Guide to...

CATS

Cartoons by Roland Fiddy

≡ EXLEY
NEW YORK · WATFORD UK

In the same series by Roland Fiddy:
The Fanatic's Guide to Computers
The Fanatic's Guide to Dads
The Fanatic's Guide to Golf
The Fanatic's Guide to Husbands
The Fanatic's Guide to Sex

First published in hardback in the USA in 1995 by Exley Giftbooks
Published in Great Britain in 1995 by Exley Publications Ltd.

12 11 10 9 8 7 6 5 4 3 2 1

Copyright © Roland Fiddy, 1994

ISBN 1-85015-636-0

Printed at Oriental Press, UAE.

Exley Publications Ltd, 16 Chalk Hill, Watford, Herts
WD1 4BN, United Kingdom.
Exley Giftbooks, 232 Madison Avenue, Suite 1206, NY 10016, USA.

②

Cats are Cacophonous

Some cats are corpulent

①

②

③

④

R-R RING!
R-R-RING!

①

②

HISSSSS!! GRRRRR!!

CUTE? WAIT TILL YOU SEE WHAT I'VE DONE IN THE BOOT!

④

③

Beware of the Dog!

Cats can be Compassionate

Cats are Curious

Cats are Clairvoyant

②

Cats can be confusing

Cats can appear contemptuou

Books in the "Crazy World" series

($4.99 £2.99 paperback)

The Crazy World of Aerobics (Bill Stott)
The Crazy World of Cats (Bill Stott)
The Crazy World of Cricket (Bill Stott)
The Crazy World of Gardening (Bill Stott)
The Crazy World of Golf (Mike Scott)
The Crazy World of The Handyman (Roland Fiddy)
The Crazy World of Hospitals (Bill Stott)
The Crazy World of Housework (Bill Stott)
The Crazy World of Love (Roland Fiddy)
The Crazy World of Marriage (Bill Stott)
The Crazy World of The Office (Bill Stott)
The Crazy World of Photography (Bill Stott)
The Crazy World of Rugby (Bill Stott)
The Crazy World of Sailing (Peter Rigby)
The Crazy World of Sex (David Pye)
The Crazy World of Soccer (Bill Stott)

Books in the "Fanatics" series

($6.99 £3.99 hardback, also available in a larger
paperback format, $4.99 £2.99)

The **Fanatic's Guides** are perfect presents for
everyone with a hobby that has got out of hand. Over
fifty hilarious colour cartoons by Roland Fiddy.

The Fanatic's Guide to Cats
The Fanatic's Guide to Computers
The Fanatic's Guide to Dads
The Fanatic's Guide to Golf
The Fanatic's Guide to Husbands
The Fanatic's Guide to Sex

Books in the "Victim's Guide" series

($4.99 £2.99 paperback)

Award-winning cartoonist Roland Fiddy sees the
funny side to life's phobias, nightmares and
catastrophes.

The Victim's Guide to the Baby
The Victim's Guide to the Christmas
The Victim's Guide to the Dentist
The Victim's Guide to the Doctor
The Victim's Guide to Middle Age

Great Britain: Order these super books from
your local bookseller or from Exley Publications
Ltd, 16 Chalk Hill, Watford, Herts WD1 4BN.
(Please send £1.30 to cover postage and packing
on 1 book, £2.60 on 2 or more books.)